Off-Leash

Off-Leash

Dorothy Mahoney

Copyright © 2016 Dorothy Mahoney
All rights reserved

Palimpsest Press
1171 Eastlawn Ave.
Windsor, Ontario. N8S 3J1
www.palimpsestpress.ca

Book and cover design by Dawn Kresan. Typeset in Adobe Garamond Pro, and printed offset on Zephyr Laid at Coach House Printing in Ontario, Canada. Edited by Dawn Kresan.

Palimpsest Press would like to thank the Canada Council for the Arts, and the Ontario Arts Council for their support of our publishing program. We also acknowledge the assistance of the Government of Ontario through the Ontario Book Publishing Tax Credit.

Library and Archives Canada Cataloguing in Publication

Mahoney, Dorothy (Anne), 1957–, author
    Off leash / Dorothy Mahoney.

Poems.
ISBN 978-1-926794-32-7 (paperback)

    I. Title.

PS8576.A446O44 2016   C811'.54   C2016-900151-2

*With love for Greg,
and Mighty Manfred, the Wonder Dog*

*Thank you to Bill and the late Sheila Trudgeon of
Woodsshadow Kennel, who were the reason, Manfred was
(and Dexter and Abbey).*

*Thank you to Dawn (Lola, Buffy and Keiko); and to
Aimee and her husband, walking Mollie by the house
every day, a reminder of daily writing.*

Dogma

- 11   Dog of Eden
- 13   Toto
- 14   Dog of Arnolfini's
- 15   Hound in Field
- 16   Argos, lament
- 17   Dog of Noah
- 18   Dog of Lot
- 19   Praise
- 20   Dog of the prodigal's brother
- 21   Kitsch dogs
- 22   City dogs
- 23   Ella in the Goodwill Bookstore
- 24   Walking, the weather
- 25   Blue Dog
- 26   Momo hiding
- 27   The last page

Just another dog

- 31   Farm dog
- 32   Charity
- 33   Stray
- 34   Pitch
- 35   Locked out
- 36   Permission
- 37   Dog deceived
- 38   Bucky
- 39   Trespass
- 40   Directions: a poem of two voices
- 44   Rat poison

45 Rin-Tin-Toke
46 Fall
47 Those
48 Litany
49 Black and White
50 Touching
51 More white
52 After work

Dog summer

55 The dog you've always wanted
56 Pick of the litter
57 Obedience class
58 On the trail
59 Sirens
60 Jiggs
61 When my friend's dog plays piano
62 When my father drew cats
64 Dog's welcome
66 Frisbees mid-air
67 Cut
68 Litter
69 Black squirrels in October
70 To name a flea Florence
71 Running with the dog
73 Death rehearsal
74 Dog years
75 Ebb
76 Space of after
77 When there's no more dog

Dogma

All knowledge, the totality of all questions and all answers is contained in the dog.

—Kafka, INVESTIGATIONS OF A DOG

Dog of Eden

Before we left—
the world without
neutering or docking,
micro-chipping or cropping.
It was skip and scamper, rolling
in the flush of it, so new, so green.
No dog breath. No dog-eat-dog.
A pure dog's life:
all run and tug, on a hill side
of lavender, basil and
thyme, before thorns and thistles,
burr and deer tick,
before crates and kennels,
alleys and garbage cans,
before the word 'beware.'
It was sun and sleep in the dimpled-
dapple of sycamore grove, easy
games of pine cone roll and acorn tumble.
Before sin and sinners, bark and biters,
melamine and windshield fluid;
it was a time of found and finding.
Sweet fruit falling from favoured trees,
we chewed on windfalls
in sweet denial of what dogs knew:
the quick slip-slither of whip-tail
and tongue.
Before choke chains and muzzles,
 before spit-turning and cart-tugging,
before bear-baiting and crowd-performing,
before chasing a mechanical hare.

We knew but did nothing
in the simple state of being.
We slept untroubled sleep.

Toto

When you're a Cairn Terrier in the witch's castle
there is much to fear:

shut in a basket,
      the winged monkey told to drown you,
            the mammoth guards, their marching feet,

the draw bridge closing,
the widening chasm
to jump.

      There's wind, smoke, fire.
          In all that is a dream:

spinning house, poppy fields,
man behind a curtain;

there's your girl lost
      on a yellow road
           with no one else to guide her.

Dog of Arnolfini's
Jan Van Eyck's *Arnolfini Wedding*, 1434

So I am fidelity, though that's not my name.
So like my master, my colouring the same.

I hide beneath tapestries, curtains and spreads.
My world is a canopy, rich- made of threads.

My mouth longs for soft kid, not shoes soled with lumber.
I search for silk scarves to entwine in my slumber.

I pirouette, an acrobat, vie for attention,
study the mistress, the master's reflection.

She dubs me the lion; I'm quick to stand guard.
My barking is regal; her finger-tip scarred.

She tempts me with sausage and lard-sopped bread.
She calls me sweet confidante, now that they've wed.

She tries hard to win me and this much is true:
I hear them approaching, not one, but still two.

Hound in Field
Alex Colville's *tempera*, 1958

This is the dichotomy of an empty field:
that there were rabbits,
that a man rendered his dog.

This the compromise of season:
patches of snow, patches of grass,
the need to run, the collared neck.

Below a horizon of dark woods—
the circling back,
a muzzle painted with hair-fine strokes,
stopped on canvas, before the train.

Argos, lament

Days multiple like fleas.
This daily rub and scratch of things.
The sun shifts shadows wide and farther.

Once I was ready for each
approaching horse, each hand nearing …
There was reason to run down the road.

How easy it seems—leave behind
what is simple, and simply forgotten,
that all might seem the same, upon return.

How all things slow under the blaze of sun.
Below a blade of grass, a bee hums.
Dozing on a dung heap, drifting into sameness.

Once I ran rabbits, felt their hind legs thrust
from their burrows, dashed and darted with deer,
through thickets I followed fear and knew swiftness.

Once I ran to his side, Odysseus, who named me,
who called and waited until I came far over fields
or just at the gate where the dung heap lies.

Now I lift my head in question—
will his voice repeat my name, his fingers rub my ears
or will the shadow of his swift step pass in my dimness.

Dog of Noah

Suddenly there is need for one more dog.
Thick sawdust becomes
bedded with urine and dung,
I tread a rush of horns and tusks, hooves and talons,
squawk and squeal of spine and snout,
the clatter of plank. The slow business of settling
into the monotony of incessant rain,
with the matter of this other dog
begging some attention.

Dog of Lot

How easy a dog for sin—
lusting dog after dog regardless,
succumbing to temptation,
devouring sausage, sandal, serpent.
A sloth for sleep.
How wrong satisfaction.

How effortless to be loyal.
Lot's wife turning back
to bid me, *Come!*

In arcing spires of smoke and sparks,
what does a dog know about redemption,
circling in all that smolders,
blindly.

Praise

Perhaps it is best not to wonder how
the dog began to dance on two legs
when the man played trumpet,
coins dropping into a hat.
To think he is happy, front legs
balancing, the tourist delights
and snaps pictures. The man nods,
one hand fingering valves,
the other with the rope
around the dog's neck.

Dog of the prodigal's brother

So much is foreseeable
like the return of birds after a season,
the kitchen maid suddenly back
after broken dishes and burnt bread,
even the wretched cat gone long ago
comes back more wretched.
Why so often in his pondering
he questioned his brother's departure,
rich in the rooster's ritual boast
of morning's revival,
his anger flaring like fat dripping
into fire.
When the fence falls,
he mends it.
When I wander,
he beckons.

Kitsch dogs

A Rottweiler between the stoic couple
of *American Gothic*, lean a
Pekinese into the arms of *Mona Lisa*, or yet,
substitute the heads of dogs for humans, or
paint by number the large-eyed dog on velvet.
There will always be dogs playing poker,
or nodding on the dashboard
of a slow-moving Chevy, a wooden
silhouette of a dog hunches over
a patchy lawn, dogs barking Christmas carols,
the bowling sweaters my mother knit
with hunting dogs and rising pheasants,
ceramic Scotties ready to shake
salt and pepper from their heads.

City dogs

Nails buffed and polished,
tucked in elbows, pockets,
designer bags, teacup and saucer,
strutting or stuffed in strollers,
coiffed and primped,
matching bows and collars,
smirking, grinning,
bling and barking,
bulldog in pearls,
high-pitched coaxing
arm candy, accessory,
gourmet biscuits,
doggie collar charms,
rhinestone sparkle,
doggles and aviator glasses,
bandanas,
diamond harness,
reversible quilted dog vest,
fleece-lined Muttluks.
Mixes and crosses:
Affenpoo, Boxerman,
Dalmadoodle,
Bulljack.
What every dog needs—
therapet and massages,
felt dog fedora,
pajamas.

Ella in the Goodwill Bookstore

On a day like this when the sun flips
the first pages of spring, the doors are wide
and she wanders in, past Romance and
beyond Adventure to Children's.
Eight and low to the ground,
she is level with the rungs of a rocker,
and the one eye of a blue rabbit.
She smells the past,
her black tail an exclamation
from the spot on her white back.
Here pages are scribbled in frantic circles,
and long leashes of crayon drag past each turning;
some with beaten covers
some never touched,
so much telling in the reverence of books.
But Ella is beyond that,
deep into Adult Fiction,
she ambles into Self-Help and Philosophy
then turns around. She has never been a connoisseur of paper,
chews all things plastic:
toothbrushes, mouth guards,
flip-flops, all things seasoned by those she loves.
Her now owner scans CD's;
she knows he will find her
like a favorite word in a monotonous passage:
melee or rumpus.
Ella is a dog for sound: her dog tags' tintinnabulation
when she hurries, the susurration of down as she
circles on the duvet, she tilts her head:
these tomes are silent,
coded like the small print of ants on sidewalk.

Walking, the weather

Duke is dead, and the man he was named after
flickers on late night TV.
They say John Wayne took the name
Duke from his Airedale;
big name, big dog.
Bud, the carpet salesman at Home Depot, tells us
his sheepdog died of a heart swelled too big,
died in his arms, a movie death scene:
heart-break and final sigh …

The times he wanted to go walking, he pulled Bud's arm,
Bud would shove him off,
 resting in his Lazy-boy.
Bud saying, *Get lost.*
Then the show-down: run, leap and
land, over one hundred pounds heavy on Bud's chest,
        to tip over
the whole chair while Bud's wife chuckled.

Duke had his own mind, a cowboy that loved rain.
He liked the feel of a strong wind.
Might've said,
Let's keep walking, this weather's fine.
Bud, no choice, grumbled
behind Duke down Main, past picture windows
of Lazy-boys and flickering Westerns.
Somewhere, small dogs slept curled
on slippers, content as horses in stables after
the stagecoach safely arrived.

Blue Dog
George Rodrigue's *Loup-Garou*, 1984

Because the dog had died,
he painted her stance from a photograph:
front legs locked with forward stare,
changed her colour to spectre-blue.
It was the silhouette—
not the cocker spaniel,
not the loup-garou of his mother's
Cajun stories.
It was shape and colour—
a massive oak, a red house,
slabs of tomb-stone pathway.
Because the dog had died,
it could be any dog,
wearing a hat and tie,
placed next to a red alligator
or a bottle of Absolut,
a dog next to a dog next to a dog.

Momo hiding
for Andrew Knapp

Behind rocks, behind trees,
behind red velvet sofas abandoned in fields,
Momo is hiding.

His red bandana a definite clue,
in wood piles, in tractors,
in shadows of barns,
where a black and white dog is not easily found.

Asleep on the seat
of the Volkswagen van,
Momo is hiding; an egg is a pebble,
a moth is a leaf, what's buried in dreams
cannot be retrieved.

The last page

After the *Births and Deaths*,
and the second cup of coffee,
it's black and white dogs in the comics:
waiting in the pumpkin patch or
flying on top of his doghouse,
a virtuoso on the typewriter.
Dogs get the last thought balloon,
or exclamation mark
like Daisy wide-awake
for the midnight *Dagwood*,
Rover helping Red with homework,
Snert barking in a Viking accent.
Every dog has his say.
As kids we lifted them
with Silly Putty, stretching them
like images in
fun-house mirrors.
Marmaduke, all legs, even longer.
Cartoon me now in my bathrobe,
their eyes alert for dog treats
drawn from my pockets.

Just another dog

> ... *sniffing the trees,*
> *just another dog*
> *among a lot of dogs. What*
> *else is there?*

—William Carlos Williams, PATERSON

Farm dog

When the old dog died, another wandered
across the cornfields and stuck around,
so she chained him to the same spot where
he drank from the same bucket, ate from
the same hubcap, slept in the same shadows,
became the old dog by his sameness,
barking at distant trucks and a fox
that would pass, seeking windfalls
beneath the crabapple.

Then, winter,
in her dead husband's jacket and boots,
she wore a path through snow,
bringing more straw from the barn,
breaking the ice like a blind eye over water,
and the dog drew nearer, ducking
under her outstretched arm, catching the chain
around her legs and she fell, the dog
down with her, whimpering, afraid.
She slumped, his tongue on her face,
finding her again.

Charity

Call them what you want but they all live together in a rundown house a few streets from the downtown liquor store. Once the monthly cheque arrives, they are strewn along the sidewalks with paper bags and bottles oblivious to the weather. It is a scorching July afternoon when they bunch around a screaming woman in a parking lot. She has left her dog in the car too long. One pulls it from the back seat, another douses it with a pail of water, a third puts his lips on the dog's mouth to draw it back.

dead fly on the sill
powders at a finger's touch—
one wing whole

Stray
for Hush

Sometimes there are calls from the police. There's a pit bull left in the house they raided. Other times it's a sighting near an empty lot, a thin dog chained to a car bumper. Armed with a net and catchpole, Carlisle and his crew retrieve the homeless, the neglected, those left behind in ditched neighborhoods of Detroit. They bring blankets, dog biscuits, and bargaining words, visit the safe houses where packs assemble, sleep on torn couch cushions, reclaiming mattresses and rooms where the rain stains the floors.

night of no moon
the dog with swaying teats
limps across the road

Pitch

There is a dog sitting at the corner. It is there all day and the next. He tells his wife. She says, *we don't need another dog*. Like another table, or another car. He opens the door and the dog settles in. They call him Max, a Bernese Mountain-husky mix. Years later, the man hammering shingles on their roof, says he once owned their dog. Thinks about getting a new one.

milkweed pod,
a discarded couch
splits a seam.

Locked out

He cowers when television voices are loud,
distances himself from food left on a low table.
The abused dog never barks,
is never persuaded.

Distances himself from food left on a low table,
hides when you come through the window;
is never persuaded
you've locked yourself out, forgotten the key.

Hides when you come through the window.
The abused dog unaccustomed to welcome.
You've locked yourself out, forgotten the key.
The abused dog suppresses the dog in himself.

The abused dog unaccustomed to welcome,
misconstrues never being beaten.
The abused dog suppresses the dog in himself,
ducks his tail between his legs or lets it lie low.

Misconstrues never being beaten;
he cowers when television voices are loud,
ducks his tail between his legs or lets it lie low.
The abused dog never tells.

Permission

I had a dog once, growing up.
A Vizsla, nice dog actually, a hunting dog,
but he was old and deaf.
I came home drunk one night and bent down
to pet him; he growled.

                     ... It wasn't his fault, really.
He must've smelled the alcohol. He bit me,
right here on the nose,
my face was full of blood.
My buddy laughed. We were both drunk.

It was hard for my mom; she loved him best.
When she had to travel, she gave me a note
that if things got bad, I had permission
to put the dog down. Ownership
was in her name. It was hard
for her, she loved that dog.
Some days I'd wave that note in his face:
Look at this! Remember?

Dog deceived

You know it will be a sad story beginning with *I just can't keep him anymore* ... as the woman tells the vet to put the dog down and leaves. You know the young assistant will fall in love, begs to keep the animal as a mascot. You know the dog settles in until the day of the open door... he runs and runs. Somehow finds his way to the house. You know he waits on the porch, curls on the welcome mat, content, knows where he belongs. You know she brings him back; but this time she stays.

Crossing the ice,
finding the dead dog
frozen beneath us.

Bucky

How much to amputate? asks my friend's husband, when the dog's hind leg was kicked by a horse. The vet assures them that the leg can be saved for a thousand dollars. *What? He's only a farm dog. I could shoot him for less.* So the vet agrees to half the price. The Jack Russell weighed down by a cast, springs at the horses with his eyes, twitches like a fishing bob tugged by a slow sturgeon. The horses, their eyes masked for flies, flick their tails, freed of one more annoyance, their giant hooves crushing the grass.

Paying a backhoe
to bury the horse
in the far field.

Trespass

His grandfather called the dog Zig. Short for gypsy, although he was steady, never drifted. The boy tempted him under the table when his grandparents weren't looking. The dog seized morsels, but backed away, weary, unwilling to be touched. *Watch him*, grandfather ordered. One afternoon in secret, the boy sails his boat across the cattle trough. Stretching and stretching, he falls face forward. Zig saves him, tugging him out by his shorts.

Open hand of oats,
luring the cow back
through the broken fence.

Directions
a poem of two voices

THE NEIGHBOUR

'Gotta minute?
Yeah, directions are easy,
name's on the mailbox.
Can't miss it!
Keep driv'n past the Arner Town Line,
you'll see a row of evergreens, their tops cut off.
That's the place.
He'll know you're comin'…
the dogs'll tell'im.
Don't worry, they're chained.
Breeds 'em, best damn huntin' dogs around.
German.
Good dogs.
Come to think of it, he's probably out huntin'…
Ever go?
A good dog does the work;
a good dog knows when to run ahead, when to fall behind;
a good dog waits.
'Know what I'm sayin'?
A good dog waits.

I saw 'im yesterday, pickin' up his wife at the train station.
Went back to the old country for a month.
Hardly ever see her.
She bakes, sells eggs.
Doesn't say much.
Puts the change in her pocket.
Know how it is? The change goes in her pocket.
'Just sayin', ain't nothin' wrong with that.

Had a real nice bitch
Said it stopped eatin' when his wife left.
Ever heard of that?
Wouldn't eat nothin',
moped around until it died.
Shame …
He threw it on the burn pile.
Know where you're goin'?
Evergreens,
evergreens with the tops cut off.

THE DOG

circle

                and

                              circle
                              circle

              and

circle

```
i could smell            her on the dish
i could smell                 her on the food
i could smell                                her
i could…
```

```
her hand                              on my head
              my head
my tongue                             on her hand
              her hand

her hand         my head        my tongue
```

her step with my step

i could smell her   on the food,   on the dish
now …

the step is   his kick   at my head
                                                    Schwine hund!

no taste   my tongue

       no smell
    no circle
no her

Rat poison

Your stupid dog is dead, yells my dad. The door slams and he leaves his farm boots on. I come running. *He ate half a bag of rat poison in the shed. How did he find that? Stupid dog!* I don't believe him and dash to the door. *Well, he's not dead yet, but will be,* he adds, as if reading my hope. I beg him to take us to the vet. He loves Sam. I know that. I know he loves me, too. I make a million promises in my heart. Just this.

rust
starburst lilies staining
the white tablecloth

Rin-Tin-Toke

He was a white shepherd that came with the house. *You'll need him; it's not a safe neighborhood,* the landlord cautioned. Sometimes the dog got out. One time he returned with a pig's head, brains and all. (Was there a butcher shop nearby?) Once while walking him on leash, a black shepherd charged. The only thing to do was let him loose. He stood his ground, clamping the other dog down at the neck. The owner ran up, cursing. *Let my dog go!* Toke secured him gently, firmly. He took care of things.

open window
the dog challenging the moon

Fall

There is a sound before the drop. That sound you can't forget, although it is so quick, and then, afterward, that hollowness. When a bird strikes the window, hard. Or, when footsteps descend the stairs too quickly and then, the end of the fall. When the car hit the dog, or the dog hit the car, we felt it. Then, there, on his side, his wide eyes looking up. Motionless. It was the hit that echoed, that squeezed us so certain we stopped breathing. It swallowed us, slammed us like a door in another room, shut fast by wind.

eggs tap-tapping
in boiling water
one bursts open

Those

Somewhere there are those
who would kick a dog
with steel-toed boots;
would laugh to hear a whimper,
to see blood on its teeth.
There are those that own fear
like a choke chain yanked fast
so a dog is robbed of breath,
use duct tape as a muzzle.
There are those who would offer
anti-freeze or rat-bait,
those who would shoot it
dead or not,
leave it twitching
on a gravel side road.

Litany

A friend put his dog in the back of a truck
before it was against the law.
Couldn't believe the dog jumped.
Didn't stop and go back after the semi hit.
Every death has its day—
farm dogs behind the barn,
graves steaming in the manure pile;
home dogs merciful on the vet's table,
interred in ceramic urns.
Just when you hope they will live forever—
killed by eating rat poison in someone else's yard,
little dogs snatched by inner-city coyotes,
missing flyers stapled to telephone poles.
Never ready for the mishap
off the overpass.
Passionate stories of devoted dogs
quietly remaining, front paws crossed on gravesites, or,
restless dogs, disappearing, reappearing in
some unexpected future.
Too soon the dog can't do stairs,
urinates on rugs,
ventures into the street
wagging his tail.
X-rays always showing what
you don't want to see:
zephyrus shadows swelling.

Black and White

When he couldn't have a dog, he got fish. Starting small with neons, then tetras, guppies and swordtails. He built tanks with panes of glass and a caulking gun. Learned about air filters, bubble nests and fin rot. He kept piranhas and fed them goldfish. But it was a dog he wanted, since before Kindergarten. Stretched on his stomach in his astronaut pajamas, watching *Tom Terrific and his Wonder Dog*, Manfred, on the black and white television. He wanted a sheepdog. There was no point naming fish.

clutch of eggs
dog hair in the nest
out of reach

Touching

It starts with another drive to the county. The farmer says, *The bitch is in heat*, as he offers pints of strawberries in spring. *There's a new litter,* as he hands them a bag of apples in fall, and always the head shake as money is exchanged. But now, this drive, with promise of the pick. *We're just checking it out, so remember, no touching!* The lure of myths, of Tantalus and the impossible stretch. Then, holding fast to the wriggle and tongue, the glossy coat and clamor, the deep eyes of the pup that became Winston.

ice off the lake
first hummer at the feeder

More white

The dog went out into the cold and then sat at the door, wanting back in. She shook herself and the floor was wet with melting snow. All morning it had been falling and had filled the tracks of the dog's wild frolics and the furtive rabbit's nightly visits around the bushes. The pruned twigs were gone. The round droppings were gone. The dog's frozen shit piles, gone. The yard was immaculate. The cement cherub in the garden, visible from the waist up, wore a white cap, her shoulders covered. Her arms were filling as if gathering snow.

luv u
white wisp of dog hair
on his black pants

After work

A dog knows your leather;
heel rubbing shoe into submission,
forcing form no one else can slip into or
fill the same way.
How one hand in a glove is not
the equal of his master's,
how hide softens, scrapes, scuffs,
pales at the seam, becomes
the familiar tread,
the known touch.

A dog anticipates
the step on the porch,
key in the lock.
The mincing
as he hunches around the kitchen,
his hard-on proclaiming his joy,
as you enter, shedding shoes and gloves,
the form of you he longs for,
that well worn touch.

Dog summer

*that of all the sights I love in this world—
and there are plenty—very near the top of
the list is this one: dogs without leashes.*

—Mary Oliver, DOG SONGS

The dog you've always wanted

You call him from another room,
the dog you've always wanted
wanders in from your childhood:
the dog that never chased cars, seldom
barked, ate but all you remember
is a rind of bologna
pulled from between white bread,
the dog that never
peed on the rug, that never
roamed far. This dog. Snapshots:
blurry by the lake, asleep against your
child-body, the close-up of his
nose and tongue, your bliss …
Still anxious to please, he comes
when you call,
the young-you eager in his eyes.

Pick of the litter

There are no runts in dogs, only pigs, she says, as the puppy nuzzles his nose into my neck. I study the others. (This one is smaller ...) My husband shoots a glance; there is no deal unless we pass this test. *Will the dog have a yard? Will he be neutered?* We nod, proceed, signing papers. She continues to praise him, *his nose is nicely filling in ...* gives a little wiggle to his chin, advises how to give his face a trim. Her husband winks, says, *people seem to like them smaller ...*

wild violets
at the children's race
everyone wins a medal

Obedience class

The poodle lunges,
straining at the leash,
panting in rasping breaths.
Pop the leash.
Give the correction.
Let 'em know who's boss.
The Dalmatian refuses
to move, lifts a leg
and streams
on his owner's leather shoes.

On the trail

It's several busy streets to the park along the river and back through to the pond, this is where you may run your dog. Here the wild aster and goldenrod surge; rabbits and pheasants rise and retreat, unseen frogs reiterate. This is where Buddy gallops, even in a storm, like today. It has been three hours and the rain, relentless. Buddy's gone. Puddles deepen and paths disappear. Even the asters drop heavy. He's nowhere. The return is hollow with *what-ifs*; the leash rattles guilt. Then, there he is, on the living room rug, dry, asleep.

walking the dog in
ever-widening circles
that start and end home

Sirens

When you're a golden retriever happy to be off leash
there is nothing like the lure of ducks, taunting, teasing, an easy float
at the edge of the lake. It is then that nothing can restrain you, hurdling

through burdock and burr, gliding past goldenrod,
thistle, milkweed, bounding into a splash

        while the ducks
                        drift from reach.

So you swim farther, legs pumping, only your head visible
with a steady focus forward unaware of the voice rippling from shore,

frantic to keep you in sight, weaving through stands of saplings.
While for you, nothing truly matters like
                                    ducks.

Jiggs

for Uncle Don, whose dog he was

Listen, there's a dog named Jiggs, needs telling about,
Aeirdale, with a squared-off head.
He was your grandfather's brother's dog, your dad's dad,
and his dad's dad, no stories left,
just a crooked shillelagh, the father kept,
and maybe, the name Jiggs, the tap of foot and stick.

Well, your dad told stories of mighty Jiggs;
the dog smacked a car and sprang right back,
followed by the driver, wanting cash for the dent.
He was a good dog, old Jiggs.

Well, Jiggs loved a doll, name of Jemima.
when old Uncle George, tried to grab her,
Jiggs gave a growl and got back Jemima.
Good dog, Jiggs! Good dog!

Late in her seventies and hard of hearing,
a neighbor said, *Hi Jake!* and Jiggs jumped to greet her.
She fell flat on the grass laughing while Jiggs licked her.
Good old Jakey Jiggs!

Once Jiggs swallowed a football bladder,
with cod-liver oil, ten doses, out-and-out passed it.
Jiggs running circles, tearing the yard up;
the joy of the jig clean sprung from his feet.
Jiggs was a dog for the telling, good old Jiggs.
Just like that. Jiggedy-Jiggedy Jiggs.

When my friend's dog plays piano

Any sweltering day you might find
the smaller dog lounging
on a rubber raft in the pool,
while CJ pilfers green peppers
from the garden on command.
This is a yard of perennial hibiscus
and raspberry-swirled tree peonies
where concrete canoes are conversation
and sugared almonds standard fare.

Buddy is the silent partner
while CJ, a mutt with inspiration,
rolls over and plays dead:
his head tossed back and legs raised
in mock stiffness
as though he had been running
in an upside-down world and was
suddenly stopped
by the word *treat*.
CJ sits silently with a dog biscuit
on his nose. A quick snap, then
sprints to the piano and throws his front
paws onto the keys.
The smaller dog ready to croon,
CJ plays a concerto only a dog could contrive.
The sound bounces like a ball.
He turns his head for applause
while the notes run like a chased squirrel
and CJ's lips curl into a smile.

When my father drew cats

When my father drew cats,
they were quick cartoons
in corners of the phone book
or newspaper margins,
triangle ears on oval heads
with "w" smiles
and whisker strokes.

When my father chose a cat
he'd always pick an orange male.
He favoured a Manx.
There was something about a bobbed tail
and high launched-back legs
for speed that would doom baby rabbits,
sparrows, field mice.

When my father named cats,
he'd say, *think of the sound,
cats don't know words.*
A name required combined
syllables unmatched in speech.
So a succession of cats
bore the name Felix.

When my father played with cats,
his nicotine-stained fingers
rolled a ball from the foil
of his Matinee pack
and he flicked it like a butt
over the cat's head.

When my father died, we had no cat
the last one replaced by a dog
that was also gone.
So I asked for a sign
and a boy came up the driveway
clutching an orange kitten
with fleas and crusted eyes
already named for a cartoon cat
and I remembered how my father drew them.

Dog's welcome

She is outside at the window
So I signal with my hand—
Come, meet me at the door, here.
She runs, her legs a tangle,
muzzle dark from mouthing
the compost lapsed into the ground.

Then up she lifts from the ground
four legs and I am a window.
She leaps and is mouthing
my neck, belt buckle, my hand.
Burrs have her fur in a tangle.
she sniffs my socks and sits here.

Well, what have we here?
Her paws have left mud ground
into my shirt and my hair a slobbered tangle
as if during a storm, a window
burst open. I rub at the stains with my hand.
Stay! But she hears other words I'm mouthing.

She is no longer puppy mouthing
leather shoes, or gnawing the baseboards here,
and her growth has my hand
reaching higher off the ground.
Her dog life a narrow window;
seasons tapping death's tangle.

She grumbles and slumps under curtains that tangle
like hems of dresses, the wind was mouthing,
Doubt like a robber climbs in through the window,
but our house is well guarded; we have a dog, here.
Her forepaws on shoulders, would bring to the ground
any stranger, licking masked face, gloved hand.

I ruffle her head with my hand,
dog dreams, a rough tangle
of catching balls mid-air, ground
rolling and sky mouthing.
On her back, asleep, it's quiet here,
the drowsy afternoon of the day's window.

My head on my hand, I'm mouthing,
the tangle of dog names to insert here—
some under rocks in the ground,
others barking at a childhood window.

Frisbees mid-air

A dog should not gambol in a gray shade of fear,
not worry his chain.
His thoughts should smell forgotten things:
a sock, a squirrel, vanilla ice cream.
When a dog runs, he must learn how to stop,
hold words, like a Frisbee caught in mid-air.
He should not bite.
This is what I tell myself.
He wants to be good.
Nights, he sleeps by the bed,
my hand floating down
forgetting if it is safe.
A stranger's words spinning:
love him until you can't.

Cut

She groomed a goat once, for a Christmas pageant, and a lion cub for a petting zoo. The dog is half-shaved and shivers in a crate near a vacuum canister she uses as a dryer. She wants us to hold him; he has snapped at her, on the table. We are like parents confronted with the delinquency of a favorite child. He licks our hands, necks, turns from her as she uses the electric razor; he barks. She continues, tells us that she has never been bitten before. At home we find nicks on his pink belly.

folded garden glove,
one finger finding
a resting bee.

Litter

You better hold on to your dog, warns the stranger. I shorten the leash and pull my friendly sheepdog closer. *Just saying. Someone's been leaving poisoned bait here at the park. Two dogs dead all ready. I'd call that murder.* He holds a trembling Chihuahua to his chest. *You've been told,* he mumbles and wanders away. Strange, I hadn't heard anything about it. My dog rushes forward to follow them. At some distance, the man bends to the ground, then I see him toss a small knotted bag to the side. I want to call him on it.

filling with air
plastic bags parachute
across the desert

Black squirrels in October

All night the squirrels gnaw at the pumpkin
on our porch, knowing the dog is asleep,
they sprint from door to tree
when car lights catch them.
Upstairs I revisit pumpkins in dream-fields,
rolling them, rolling them,
thudding monsters across dried stubble.
And how like a nightmare it evolves,
a gaping hole like a constant scream.
It makes me step back from the mailbox
stretching for the morning paper over
disemboweled flesh and scattered seeds.

To name a flea Florence
for Matt

My science teacher once said
that fleas do not bite humans;
I disagreed but he would not listen.
A flea can jump four thousand lengths its size,
or something like that.
A reddish purple welt
erupting on my ankle.

Our puppy nibbles at his leg
rapidly back and forth
as if it were a corn cob,
and I search his wet fur
for a darting black speck
I name Florence.

The best way to kill a flea:
pull it apart with thumbnails
pressed against the forefinger.
The long hind legs
quiver, eager to jump.

Running with the dog

> *the river called to mind*
> *a dog's docile tongue*
> *or a dog's sad belly*
> *or that other river*
> —Joao Cabral de Melo Neto
> LANDSCAPE OF THE CAPIBARIBE RIVER

The night comes faithful
and street lights
turn the autumn maples
into yellowing chandeliers.
The dog speeds ahead
to sniff each trunk, each
garbage pail and post
until I pass and chide her;
my echoing words unheeded as if it were
the river called to mind.

Through the drift of leaves
we are fleeting witness to:
a neighbor's muffled quarrel,
a skunk's
sudden stop,
a smoker on an unlit porch,
a cat paused on a roof.
Someone is burning wood,
the smell a remembered solace like
a dog's docile tongue.

I begrudge this walk in the rain, or
when the sidewalk goes icy,
and if I come home late,
how easy it is not to walk,
thrust the dog into the yard
and slam the door.
But this night now is a raft
with only us two in a settled course,
no burrs to hook our passage
or a dog's sad belly.

She starts to slow
for a stooped recliner moored
at the curb, hesitates, I steer her along;
there are no stars even at the
burnt out street light,
this dimness with an ashen glow.
We're almost home, I say;
want to linger
not ready for the next season
or that other river.

Death rehearsal

My flashlight shines a circle on death
as the dog's delirious barking brings
me to the darkest corner of the yard.
I hold her back by the collar
as she lunges forward challenging
the stiff opossum, its tight teeth clamped
in a grimace at being caught, posed like some taxidermist's
dream, balanced like a tightrope walker
between breath and no breath, its eyes a solemn stare,
its long tail a shoelace. I know she would run with it,
throw it into the air like a flattened football or
stolen slipper, unwilling to relinquish what she has found.
 But I tug her back inside.
Later she will reclaim the empty spot, confused,
while the possum, risen,
will remember only
a tunnel of light and a voice commanding it to stay.

Dog years

You are the reminder of my mortality,
pulling me along
as you race ahead
advancing beyond my own age
in dog years
to reach the end of your lead
to fall behind
when I have settled completely
into step with you.

That there might be others
seems startling now,
that I am the witness of your age
marking time with your name

before you …

and after …

How many of my own years have I myself forgotten
yet you marked mornings by meals and walks
when only the sun was waking.

I hurried
while you lingered wistfully
at each tree and corner watchful-
wary of what I could not see.

Ebb

We bury the dog near the gate where he most liked to sit. The ground is a root of knots from a nearby poplar and grief digs the shovel hard. The next spring is wet and false morels surface like spongy brains, lobed and mottled.

under the Colosseum
exotic seeds
from the manes of lions

Space of after
for Foster who drooled

Somewhere across fallow fields of cirrus clouds
run ghost dogs: wisps of their withers, haunches and hock;
pads of their paws; scrawl of nails skidded on sky.

Listless day of mindless duties minus panting and dripping tongue
more than absence or missing, the void of gone
the silence that makes you stare at clouds.

Later, taking the garbage cans to the curb,
there is no silhouette at the door, at the gate,
no bark beckons, no tail wags for your return, a vacant house.

Somewhere beyond the night sheen of urban heavens,
the solace of stars, constellation of dogs, *Major* and *Minor*,
distant barking, dog in darkness. Dog Star.

When there's no more dog

The gate is left open
and the flowerbeds are intact.
Squirrels have no need for detours,
seldom run along the tops of fences,
convene in the middle of the yard to chew acorns,
dig uninterrupted.
Sparrows long for the dog bowls,
the dry pebble of food
gone stray between the patio stones.

No need to check the yard,
no more barking at night,
no sense of urgency in
the woodlot
where the grass
refuses to grow even without
the daily crisscross of padded feet,
no matted fur or mud,
no worried piece of stick gnawed
to the center,
no need to close the gate.

Acknowledgements

Some of these poems, or earlier versions of them, have appeared in the following print and on-line journals: *Descant, Drabler, Haibun Today,* Leaf Press' *Monday Poem, Modern Haiku, The Dalhousie Review,* and *Wattpad.* "Dog Years" received second prize in Cranberry Tree Press' poetry contest and was anthologized in *Ellipsis* (Cranberry Tree Press, 2008). The haiku from the haibun "Charity" was published in Leaf Press' *Leaflet Series* (2014).

Thank you to all who shared their dogs and their stories especially: Pat (Bear), Ellen (Foster), Hazel (Bucky), Karen (Logan), Dave (Taz), Karen (Sasha), Barb (Buddy and C.J.), Bonnie (Sam), Colin (Buddy), Mike (Toke), Paul (Winston), Michael (Zig.), Richard (Max), Tonya, Andrew Knapp and his dog Momo in his photographs and book, Finding Momo, and Daniel 'Hush' Carlisle of Detroit Dog Rescue, and those who believe in dogs.

Special thanks to Terry Ann Carter who lives and breathes haiku, and kept pointing me to the moon, gently and with generous friendship. Thank you for the wild violets. To Lenore and the Glenairley writers, who encouraged the dogs. And thank you to Max Marshall who knows jigs.

Author Biography

Dorothy Mahoney is the author of two poetry collections, *Through Painted Skies* and *Returning to the Point*. Her poetry has been included in numerous anthologies, most recently appearing in *Detours: An Anthology of Poets from Windsor and Essex County*. A retired teacher, she resides in Windsor, Ontario.

PHOTO CREDIT: Matthew Mahoney